"As a coach of women's volleyball, I have a passion for girls making wise relationship decisions. After receiving and reading a copy of *Letters to My Daughters* I was so impressed that I asked all the girls in our church's youth group to buy a copy so they could study it." —High School JV Coach

"I have used *Letters to My Daughters* with a number of my college athletes. It is so special because the letters were originally written for just Paul's daughters. The book is therefore very personal and a powerful encouragement for young women as they navigate through the challenges of dating and marriage." —Jill Perry
Staff Member, Fellowship of Christian Athletes, Athens, Georgia

"As a dad to two daughters, the wisdom, counsel, and insight that Paul shares caused me to read *Letters to My Daughters* a second time. The third time I read this book was with a group of seven 12th grade boys in a small bible study group. Paul's questions for each letter generated laughter, great discussions, and self-examination as these young men looked to their future and the husbands they want to be one day. I look forward to reading it again with my own son as he enters his high school years." —Scott Gregerson
Visalia, California

"We had enjoyed reading *Letters to My Daughters* individually and were excited to use the *Discussion Guide* with a group of high school students from our church. The interest level in these resources has been evidenced by the enthusiasm, consistent participation, and lively discussion of the teens in our group. It has been great to see these students wrestle with scriptural principles regarding God's design for relationships." —Dan and Lois Frasier
Boxford, Massachusetts

"We have now distributed seven cases of *Letters to My Daughters* at our local schools. *Letters to My Daughters* has become invaluable for some of the junior high girls to ward off the peer pressure to participate in activities that make them uncomfortable." —Joseph Forrester
Upper Peninsula Christians, Inc., Cedarville, Michigan

"As a dad of two high-school daughters, I have found *Letters to My Daughters* to be a powerful and thought-provoking book—one that any age woman should read as they consider what is important in dating relationships and eventually marriage. It has been a pivotal tool to help my daughters and others to create priorities and boundaries as they decide what they desire in a husband. As a pastor overseeing youth and adults, I look forward to the many discussions this guide will foster. I strongly recommend this *Discussion Guide* for individuals and for small group studies." —Johnie Moore
Pastor of Discipleship/Training, Golden Hills Community Church
Brentwood, California

Letters to My Daughters

Discussion Guide

Paul A. Friesen

LETTERS TO MY DAUGHTERS: DISCUSSION GUIDE
Paul A. Friesen

Copyright © 2012 by Paul A. Friesen
Cover design: Michael Benes, Barbara Steele, Christine Kerns
Interior design and production: Barbara Steele, Christine Kerns
Copyediting: Guy Steele

ISBN: 978-1-936907-00-7

Home Improvement Ministries
209 Burlington Road, Suite 105
Bedford, MA 01730

Find us on the web at: www.HIMweb.org

First printing, April 2012
Printed in the United States of America.   4/10-12TPS2K

Contents

Foreword

Letters to My Daughters is absolute gold! It is on my short list of "must read books." I am thrilled that Paul Friesen is now offering a companion discussion guide to enhance and expand the usefulness of the letters he wrote his daughters back when they were in high school and college and then generously shared with all of us.

Six years ago I wrote the foreword to that book, *Letters to My Daughters*. I was excited about how God might use the book, but had little knowledge about how well He would lead me to use it in my own life and ministry. However, in these past six years, I have:

- given *Letters to My Daughters* to each of my own four children (two sons and two daughters),
- repeatedly told my church of 10,000 that every parent of every teen should buy this book for their kids and have them read it,
- directed all our high school leaders to read it, and finally,
- have found it helpful to put my coffee mug on to protect our coffee table while watching sporting events.

The new *Discussion Guide* you are now holding will be invaluable to you as you ponder more fully the truths of each letter in *Letters to My Daughters*. For small groups, the questions in this *Discussion Guide* will foster lively discussion that will help each of you think together about how best to apply the truths of the letters in your present relationships. For pastors and youth leaders, it will be an additional tool in your relationship-building tool box as you seek to help teens and parents discuss the building of God-honoring relationships.

God-honoring marriages start with God-honoring decisions regarding relationships. I believe the truths of God's word expressed in this book will encourage and equip you to this end.

Ray Johnston, Senior Pastor
Bayside Church
Granite Bay, CA

Introduction

We all face choices each day and regularly make decisions that will affect our lives to one degree or another. There are two decisions, however, that will affect our lives more than any other.

The first decision has to do with our response to Jesus Christ and the relationship we will have with Him. This decision is hands down the most important decision we will ever make and will affect many of our day-to-day decisions, and in fact will determine our eternal destiny.

The second most important decision of our lives is whether, and if so whom, we will marry. Someone once said being married to the right person is the closest thing we will experience to heaven on earth, and being married to the wrong person is the closest thing we will experience to hell on earth. I do know from my own life and the observation of thousands of other couples that whom we marry will basically influence every area of our life and the joy we experience. This is not a decision we should enter into lightly.

The discussion guide you hold in your hands has 52 chapters, corresponding to each of the 52 letters in *Letters to My Daughters*. Each chapter has a verse of scripture that goes along with the subject matter of the letter, followed by a vignette written by a reader in response to each letter. Names have not been included for privacy reasons, but each person, whether single, married, divorced, or widowed, wrote honestly from his or her heart about the subject of the letter. Each chapter concludes with a list of questions for discussion or reflection.

How to Use This Guide

This guide was designed to be as flexible and adaptable as you need it to be.

- Use it as a personal daily guide to go deeper into the matters covered in each letter.
- Use it as a 52-session discussion guide for a small group.
- Use the eight-week study as a guide for a two-month weekly study.
- Customize the guide by choosing particular letters you want to focus on each week and asking participants to read ahead.

Our desire is that this discussion guide will foster further communication on the critically important topic of whom to marry.

Some Memories...
Some Dreams

Philippians 3:12

Not that I have already obtained all this, or have already been made perfect, but I press on to take hold of that for which Christ Jesus took hold of me.

The story is told of former President Bill Clinton and his wife Hillary visiting the town they grew up in. As they drove by a gas station, Hillary mentioned that before she married Bill, she had almost married the man who now owned the gas station. "Just think," Bill said, "if you had done that, you would be married to a mechanic!" "Honey," replied Hillary, "*if I had married him, he would be the President of the United States.*"

The choice of whom you marry will deeply affect the rest of your life.

1. Cite an example of a poor choice you have made in the past that you are now embarrassed about or wish had never happened.

2. How will the decision about whom you marry impact all aspects of your life?

3. The author writes, "the real purpose of the letters to follow is to put on paper some thoughts regarding the second most important decision of life: marriage" (p. 14). Do you believe that whom you decide to marry is the second most important decision you'll ever make? Why or why not? How might your response to Christ be important to the question of whom you eventually marry?

4. What are some of the traits, characteristics, and attributes you would like to find in the man or woman you might marry some day?

5. In what ways might singleness be a "better gift" than marriage for a person?

The Second Most Important Decision

1 Kings 11:4

As Solomon grew old, his wives turned his heart after other gods,
and his heart was not fully devoted to the Lord his God,
as the heart of David his father had been.

"It's hard to imagine the scope of the truth of this letter before you get married, in part because as humans we're so "here and now" oriented and in part because of our propensity for believing the fairy tale that we'll live "happily ever after" no matter what. I'm sure I had no idea, really, of how true it would be in my life 35 years ago when I got married, but if I had one wish for all unmarried couples, it would be that they would take really seriously the idea that the marriage decision will affect every area of their lives—even if the marriage doesn't last. I am a much better person today because of the man I married, and that's because first, he's committed to the Lord, and second, he's committed to loving me well. These things were true of him before we got married, and he has just grown more into the man I saw he was premaritally. In addition to my assessment of him, it was really important to me that the people who knew me well and whose opinion I most respected also saw what I saw in him. Though far from perfect, our marriage has allowed us to be better together, and by His grace, it has been life-giving to others."

1. What do you think contributes to whether or not a married couple will experience a vital marriage?

2. How would you describe the mate your dad and/or mom would choose for you if the choice were up to them? How would their choice be similar or different from the person you are now dating or envision marrying some day?

3. How does the word of God affect your relationship decisions?

4. What qualities in a spouse are you looking for in order to do everything possible to avoid becoming another divorce statistic?

5. The author emphasizes to his daughters that they must first find intimacy with Christ (p. 18). What happens when we expect romantic relationships to fill a void that only Christ can fill? How can you grow your intimacy with Christ today?

Jetta Trip—
Not Like It Used to Be

Psalms 119:105

Your word is a lamp to my feet and a light for my path.

"People driving along the roads of life today are traveling at very high speeds in the area of sexuality. I drove off-road for more than half of my 26-year-old life. It has been at great cost: I've had inordinate emotional intimacy; had a past of multiple sex partners; went down paths of sexual wickedness; though curable, was marked with a sexually transmitted disease; and had a child out of wedlock. Reading this letter, I think about all the wisdom that's here. It makes me think of a phrase we as people say: "If I only knew then what I know now." Although it's only a phrase, boy, is it true! The things that I've done stay with me and on a continual basis pop in my head. Christ is just and faithful and has forgiven me of my sins. (1 John 1:9) And I am a new creation, all things are new; the old is past and the new is here! (2 Corinthians 5:17) Hallelujah! However, I do wish for you a life free from the injuries I sustained from driving off the road."

1. How do you think the area of relationships has changed since your parents were dating? What has contributed to that change?

2. What are some of the additional pressures teens experience today in the area of relationships?

3. Besides the risks of sexually transmitted diseases, what do you feel are reasons for not becoming sexually involved with someone outside of marriage today?

4. Describe someone you know who has obeyed God's "road signs" in the area of relationships. How has it affected his or her life?

5. Do you truly believe that God's design for sexual involvement exclusively inside the gift of marriage is better than what the world suggests about sex and marriage? Why, at times, is it so hard to trust that God's ways are better than ours?

Convictions

Character
Considerations
Chemistry

This is the most critical area in a relationship, and yet, often, the most overlooked. Having a shared faith and agreement on the ultimate authority in one's life will ultimately determine your response to many, many decisions as well as how you face difficulties in marriage.

What faith do you wish to participate in as a couple? And if you have children, in what faith do you wish to raise them? Prior to marriage, it is easy to ignore such subjects, saying, "we will work that out after we are married," or, "it won't be hard, we love each other." This may seem true at the time, but when it comes to where you worship, it is important to make sure you are aware of the importance you each put on this before you tie the knot.

What is your ultimate authority for how you make life decisions? If scripture is the ultimate authority for one and not the other, huge issues may arise. One person, committed to scripture, may say, "We need to tithe, giving 10% of our money to the church." The one not committed to scripture will say, "Are you crazy? I work hard for that money and I don't plan to give it away to some church." It may show itself in how you spend your weekends. Will being involved in your church be a pattern you have and continue?

When difficulties come in marriage and you are not experiencing the happiness you thought marriage would bring, do you rely on scripture's admonition not to divorce but to work at oneness— or will you or your partner pursue our culture's advice to find your own personal happiness above all else?

A Man Whole Without You

Colossians 2:9–10a, NASB

For in Him all the fullness of Deity dwells in bodily form,
and in Him you have been made complete . . .

"As a female, I think we sometimes get into this desperate state where we begin to compromise on our choice in men, and maybe settle for less than we had prayed for and expected in a mate. This letter validated my feelings about waiting for a man who is complete prior to being in a relationship with someone. I love the emphasis that two wholes become one, not two halves. Though marriage is a source of great joy and spiritual growth, it is so important to have full confidence in who we are in Jesus before we enter into marriage. It sounds odd, but it seems we really are not ready for marriage unless we are content as singles."

1. Why does scripture make such a big deal about Christians only marrying those who are also following Christ as well? (2 Corinthians 6:14) Is this important to you? Why or why not?

2. Since scripture never talks about dating, let alone whether or not you should date a non-believer, how do you make the decision of "unequally yoked" in regards to dating? What are the risks of dating someone with a different belief system?

3. Isn't it romantic to have someone say to you, "Without you in my life, my life has no meaning" or something of that sort? Why might this be a scary rather than romantic sentiment?

4. What are some practical ways that we can become more "whole" with Christ rather than depending on a significant other to take on this responsibility?

5. Describe a couple you know who are madly in love with each other, but don't seem to "need" each other to exist or function fully.

5

Do You Share a Love for God?

2 Corinthians 6:14

Do not be yoked together with unbelievers.
For what do righteousness and wickedness have in common?
Or what fellowship can light have with darkness?

"I certainly knew the term "unequally yoked" when I got married. I just wish I'd had an image of what it might mean down the line to be unequally yoked. While I was dating (and even after I married), I couldn't foresee a time when it would *really* come into play. Everything was fine and we were so happy together. Couldn't we believe different things and still love each other? Every marriage eventually hits very difficult/discouraging times. When that time came for us, it suddenly became very clear to me how the "unequally yoked" difference came into play. Because we didn't turn together to the same source for hope, encouragement, and guidance, we turned against each other. I could see how couples that loved the Lord together faced their challenges in an entirely different way and it was only then I could see what I'd missed by my choice."

1. What are some signs of spiritual vitality to look for in someone who you might be interested in?

2. What are some common reasons why Christians might compromise by being in a relationship with someone who does not share their same faith?

3. How might your relationship with the Lord be affected by your dating—and/or eventually marrying—someone who does not share your passion for Christ?

4. Since seriously dating someone who is not a believer seems to be a high risk, what are some ways to relate to those who have no relationship with the Lord and yet have an interest in you?

5. Describe a couple that are dating or married that seem to share a passion for Christ. Is that a relationship you desire to have some day? What will make that more likely to be a reality?

6

Priorities Are Best Seen...
Not Talked About

Proverbs 26:11

As a dog returns to its vomit, so as fool repeats his folly.

"Actions speak louder than words. Look to a man's actions and to his habits to see what type of man he is. Who is he when he is not with you, when "no one is looking"? Character is how he treats the people he does not know or does not like. I remember how good a young man looked based on his application to work at our Christian camp. Then we "friended" him on Facebook. His profile picture showed him drinking with his friends and his "wall" was as vulgar as underpass graffiti. Look for what a man has poured his life into, not what he *says* he will. "

1. What are some ways you are able to detect a person's true priorities in life?

2. How do you detect whether there is a discrepancy between what someone says and what he truly believes?

3. What would make a girl believe her boyfriend's promise to support her after they are married even though he has never had a steady paying job?

4. What are some indications that a man or woman has a true priority to grow in his or her Christian walk? What are some practical ways to see what his or her faith is really like?

5. Name a man you really admire who has clearly made the choice to center his life around his relationships with the Lord, his wife, and his family.

Does He Love God's Word?

Psalms 119:9

How can a young man keep his way pure?
By living according to your word.

❝One of the best ways my husband led me while we were dating was in his passion for God's word. I could not get an hour into my day without him sending me some scripture that had spoken to him that morning. He was constantly washing me in scripture and challenging me to dwell on its truth all throughout my day. During times of stress, frustration, and even rejoicing, he always supported me and encouraged me through scripture. He was so disciplined in starting each day with time with the Lord and it has been so sweet and challenging to see this discipline continue in marriage.❞

1. What role has the word of God played in your parents' marriage?

2. Why is your future spouse's view on scripture so critical?

3. Though no two people will believe the same regarding every theological issue found in scripture, what are some doctrines you believe are essential to agree on?

4. What are practical indicators that might give you insight into someone's true conviction towards scripture before you marry him or her?

5. Describe an experience where you saw a couple put their allegiance to scripture ahead of what would have been easier or what was generally expected from culture.

8

Is He Glad to Go to the House of the Lord?

Hebrews 10:25

*Let us not give up meeting together, as some are in the habit of doing,
but let us encourage one another—
and all the more as you see the Day approaching.*

"When we were dating, we decided we would find a denomination we would both be comfortable with as a couple to share our faith and eventually raise our family. Because we were never really on the same page, it became more difficult in the marriage. Over time, I grew deeper in my walk with Christ and loved being in God's house, with His people, and my husband did not, thus creating tension between us. I was naive in dating and did not realize how different our convictions on faith were. I had just assumed he would desire to grow deeper and live out our faith in more meaningful ways. I wish I had taken more seriously his casualness toward being in God's house, with His people."

1. Why is being deeply connected to a local church important to your growth as a Christian? Is it important to you? Why or why not?

2. How might being disconnected from a church family be detrimental to your marriage?

3. Should it trouble you when your significant other says that he or she prefers being in relationship with those who do not follow Christ rather than those that do? Why or why not?

4. How can relationships within the body of Christ protect you from a failing marriage?

5. What are some practical steps to take if the person you are dating isn't interested in attending church?

9

Don't Marry out of Desperation or Pity

Song of Solomon 8:7

Many waters cannot quench love; rivers cannot wash it away.
If one were to give all the wealthy of his house for love,
it would be utterly scorned.

"When I was a little girl I dreamed of my prince charming. He of course was perfect and swept me off my feet :). I also dreamed that I would go to college, graduate with a beautiful diamond on my finger, get married soon after, and live happily ever after. I am now 28 (quickly closing in on 29) and am in a *very* single stage of life. There have been many times over the last few years when I have been frustrated with my situation. Why hasn't God given me that man with whom I can share my life? It can be tempting at times to want to lower my standards and to desire a relationship more than God's best for my life. This letter has been helpful in reminding me how important it is to wait for the man that God has for me—not merely a man, but someone with whom I can share my adventure, someone who will pursue dreams and seek God with me. I believe he is worth waiting for and that God is big enough to fill my dreams."

1. How has the marriage of your parents affected your view of marriage?

2. Is there ever such a thing of having too high standards when it comes to whom you marry? How can you find out if your standards are too high or unrealistic?

3. What might cause someone to "settle" for a spouse who is less than what she or he had always imagined?

4. What does the phrase "in love with love" mean to you?

5. It what ways is it better to be single than to be married to the wrong person?

Character

Convictions

Considerations

Chemistry

Character is really the living out of one's convictions. Someone once said, "Character is who you are when no one is looking." You should observe carefully who this person is when he is not trying to impress you or anyone else. How does he treat the cashier who is annoying and he will never see again? Is the person you are involved with honest? Is he kind? Does he like to serve others? Or is this person rather selfish? Is he generous and hospitable? Is he comfortable with who he is and "whole" in his relationship with Christ? Has he "left home" and able to function independently? Does he have a good work ethic? His character should make you thankful for the person he is now and confident of who he will be in the years to come.

The Four Seasons Rule

2 Samuel 13:12–15

"Don't, my brother!" she said to him. "Don't force me. Such a thing should not be done in Israel! Don't do this wicked thing. What about me? Where could I get rid of my disgrace? And what about you? You would be like one of the wicked fools in Israel. Please speak to the king; he will not keep me from being married to you." But he refused to listen to her, and since he was stronger than she, he raped her. Then Amnon hated her with intense hatred. In fact, he hated her more than he had loved her. Amnon said to her, "Get up and get out!"

"I once dated someone for 10 months. We had been friends in college and entered our relationship prayerfully. The first 6 months were bliss. We loved being together, we talked about everything, and we were honoring God with our physical relationship. However, a few days after our 6-month anniversary, my boyfriend told me he wasn't sure he believed in God after all. I was shocked, but so thankful we hadn't gotten engaged after those few great months, like many of our friends were doing. We were just dating, so we had the freedom to end our relationship, which was best for both of us. People change, trials happen, and it takes time to truly get to know someone. Four seasons is a good time frame to date someone before talking of marriage so you more fully know the person and thus marry with confidence!"

1. How have you seen other couples relationships impacted by committing too early or by waiting too long to commit? What do you feel should go into the decision of when it is right to commit to each other?

2. What are some of the reasons a couple might commit to each other after only a very short time of knowing each other?

3. What are some ways you can "slow down" a relationship to give you more time to get to know each other more fully?

4. What are the risks and benefits of adhering to the four-season rule before committing to each other?

11

He's Got to Leave
Before He Can Cleave

Genesis 2:24

*For this reason a man will leave his father and mother
and be united to his wife, and they will become one flesh.*

"I was initially glad my husband seemed to have a close relationship with his parents, as I came from a broken home, but I later discovered he had never really separated from them as an adult. This became a problem in the marriage because his family expected to be first in his life. We did marital counseling, which helped him set healthy boundaries for a while. However, because of his need to please his parents at all costs, he was never able to put our marriage above what his parents wanted."

1. What does the phrase "leave his father and his mother, and be joined to his wife" teach about the process of getting married?

2. Why do you think God gave the directive to leave mother and father to Adam and Eve, even though they had no earthly parents?

3. How could a tight-knit family of origin be a challenge or a blessing in the early years of marriage?

4. How do you think can tell before marriage whether a man has "left home?" What are practical ways that a man should be leaving home?

5. Describe a couple that seems to have a close relationship with each other and with their parents.

12

How Important Is Your Family's Opinion?

Genesis 24:1–4

Abraham was now old and well advanced in years, and the LORD had blessed him in every way. He said to the chief servant in his household, the one in charge of all that he had, "Put your hand under my thigh. I want you to swear by the LORD, the God of heaven and the God of earth, that you will not get a wife for my son from the daughters of the Canaanites, among whom I am living, but will go to my country and my own relatives and get a wife for my son Isaac."

“My parents and brother love God and love me with the overflow of His love in their lives. We have a very close relationship (something that might later make it hard to cleave!). When I started dating my first boyfriend, I desperately wanted them to love each other. While they were all kind to him, I could tell they had some reservations about whether he was right for me. Late one night on a drive home to our parents' house, my brother gently brought up some concerns he was seeing in our relationship and questioned whether my boyfriend was right for me. I was upset and argued with him about what he didn't see, how unaccepting he was, and how my boyfriend was different, but not bad for me. Eventually I came to see that my brother was right, and I am now so thankful for his boldness in giving me his opinion, which I know was out of an incredible love for me. While I was too blind to see the ways my boyfriend wasn't right for me, my brother and parents provided loving eyes to help me get out of an unhealthy relationship. I know they know to some degree what's best for me. ”

1. If you are called to "leave" mother and father, why should you be concerned with what your families think of your marriage?

2. In what situations do you feel it is justified to go against your parents' wishes?

3. Why might it be very beneficial to listen to the concerns of your parents before marriage?

4. How might our family's backgrounds affect our marriage even if they are both supportive of the relationship?

5. How have you seen extended families influence couples you know?

Is He a Leader?

Ephesians 5:25

Husbands, love your wives,
just as Christ loved the church and gave himself up for her . . .

"When my husband and I started dating, we were sophomores in high school. On our second date, he asked me if I believed in Jesus, because he would not consider becoming serious and marrying anyone who was not a Christian. On our fourth date he told me he was not going to have sex until he was married and if I wasn't ok with that the relationship was over. He led us in our relationship for the next 7 years and we were able to keep our pledge to the Lord and each other of sexual purity. I feel badly for so many women who need to take the lead in sexual standards and spiritual pursuits. Now that we are married, he continues to lead us spiritually in our own times of reading and prayer. I don't know what our future holds, but I am confident my husband will continue to rely on God's word as his final authority and lead us as a family."

1. Describe your ideas of leadership in a relationship. Does allowing a man to lead in a relationship mean that a woman doesn't contribute to that relationship in any sort of leadership role?

2. What are some practical ways that men can lead in a relationship? What are some practical ways that women can let their husbands lead?

3. How might a "yes, dear" husband fail to love his wife as Christ loved the church?

4. In the area of sexual boundaries, how have you seen men in your life show leadership?

5. Describe a man that you have seen lead his wife and family in a God-honoring way. What strikes you about this man, his marriage, and his family?

Is He a True Servant?

Mark 10:45

*For even the Son of Man did not come to be served, but to serve,
and to give his life as a ransom for many.*

❝I couldn't have imagined when we were just starting out how grateful I would later be to have married someone with a servant's heart. Helping others is part of what makes my husband who he is, and boy, have I benefited from this attitude over the years! Whether it was gently apologizing for getting the wrong frozen vegetables (how could we have foreseen that the first months of pregnancy would turn me into a stranger who cried when confronted with carrots?!) or always being willing to recognize an overtired/overstressed mama and get to work helping out (even after a very long day at work himself), he does these things naturally and joyfully. Our neighbors and friends and family would all testify to his servant attitude, and I will testify to the fact that after all these years it is still a very attractive quality to observe in him (ahem, I guess that thought would go with the letter on marital chemistry!).❞

1. What comes to mind when you hear the word "servant"?

2. Whom does the word "servant" represent most clearly in your family of origin? Explain.

3. What are some practical ways you could discern the "servant quotient" in your boyfriend or girlfriend? Why should the man be the chief servant?

4. Christ came as the chief servant. Husbands are to love their wives as Christ loved the church. How might Christ's example be expressed in relationships today?

5. Describe a marriage where you feel the husband has modeled exemplary servanthood.

15

A Selfish Mate Is Worse Than No Mate at All

Matthew 20:28

". . . just as the Son of Man did not come to be served, but to serve, and to give his life as a ransom for many."

"I got to know my husband on a missions trip in Africa many years before we even considered being more than friends. I remember recognizing his heart for serving the materially poor and how hard he was working to help them build structures to house their small businesses. He is a very handy man and he was using the talents God gave him to serve those in need. I remember admiring his heart for God, and I knew it was something I should be looking for in a mate, but I wasn't ready yet to receive it. Years later, once I had finally figured out that my poor relationship choices were only leading me to heartache and pain, what started as a friendship grew into something so beautiful and so beyond what I could have asked for or imagined . . . It seemed to be just as God designed it to be. I did feel like a princess, and I still do after 6 years of marriage! It is so worth waiting for!"

1. In what areas do you struggle with selfishness the most?

2. How are you able to detect a selfish spirit in another?

3. Without naming names, describe the most selfish person you have gone out with or know. What made that person come across as extremely selfish?

4. Practically speaking, in what ways can selfishness destroy relationships?

5. How did Christ model unselfishness? How should imitating Christ affect our relationships?

Don't Assume He'll Mature

1 Timothy 5:22

*Do not be hasty in the laying on of hands, and
do not share in the sins of others. Keep yourself pure.*

Prior to meeting my husband, I recall a consistent theme in dating: "he will be great in 5 years . . ." or "he would be perfect if only . . ." I believe these thoughts cross most of our minds as we wait for God's best for us. The truth is, in many of those relationships, we are waiting for one more quality that we desire or believe that time will bring. The missing piece for me was often the maturity factor or the vision for service. It became clear as I dated great guys that this was not just a preference I could grow accustomed to, this was part of my heart and a part of me I wanted to see in my future husband. This meant saying goodbye to quality guys; however, I believed in my heart that if God plants a calling and desire in your heart which is of Him, it is His greatest desire to bless you with a spouse that shares that passion. The truth is none of those guys would have been poor choices, but I did not feel that they were God's best. Many may view you as crazy to let a great guy go, but I can confidently say, since I am married to a man whose heart understands mine, that it is worth waiting for God's best.

1. Why do we often make excuses or overlook the flaws in those we are dating?

2. What practical steps can you take in addressing character issues with your significant other?

3. What steps are you willing to take if certain changes are not met within a reasonable timeline?

4. What are some signs of a maturing Christian? How long do you think you should wait to confirm whether a "change" is real?

5. How do you think the author' wife's knowledge of his being "neatness challenged" before marriage might have affected her regarding marriage?

What's His Self-Control Quotient?

Galatians 5:22–23

But the fruit of the Spirit is love, joy, peace, patience,
kindness, goodness, faithfulness, gentleness and self-control.
Against such things there is no law.

"While we were dating, my husband had an occasional hot temper over minor incidents and sometimes could say mean things. He would immensely apologize and do grand things to make up for his behavior. After our marriage, he showed less self-control over his temper and anger issues, as he no longer needed to impress me. What I did not realize was that his behavior was actually very familiar and comfortable because of my own childhood, even though I had declared I wanted a very different husband and family life for myself. It is worth repeating to say that looking at past performance both prior to and during the dating relationship is usually an indicator of future behavior. "

1. What are some areas in which you could see lack of self-control affecting a marriage?

2. In what ways does our culture lessen the value of self-control in individuals and relationships? Why isn't self-control a virtue that is valued in our culture?

3. Why do you suppose self-control is included in the "Fruit of the Spirit"? Why is God honored by men and women who are growing in self-control?

4. If you are dating, what areas of self-control concern you about the person you are dating?

5. Describe an individual or couple who exhibit self-control. How have you seen it affect them in a positive manner?

18

I'm Glad He Loves Jesus, but Does He Have a Job?

1 Timothy 5:8

If anyone does not provide for his relatives, and especially for his immediate family, he has denied the faith and is worse than an unbeliever.

"I laughed at this title—however, it is very important. Sometime we want a relationship so badly we cling to the promises of a man, such as, "God will provide," or "All we really need is love." I am a child of divorce and a sibling of someone who has divorced because of financial issues. I have seen money destroy two marriages. Women get caught up in the dreams and hopes of what a man says he wants to do, often neglecting to look at his track record in the area of work.

I remember a man asking me out for lunch and then splitting the check. As we were leaving he said, "This was great—could we do this again?" "No, I don't think so," was my reply.

I want a man who does not depend on me to pay our way. If he has not been able to manage his money by now, I doubt he will all of a sudden become financially "responsible." "

1. What benefit might there be in the husband taking the primary role of providing for the family?

2. How would you like being married to a guy who is relaxed about you being the "income producer" in the family? What might be some of the challenges?

3. How can you know what kind of a provider he might be if your whole experience of knowing each other has been in school?

4. Is it the husband's responsibility to make as much money as possible? How might being overly concerned with providing for your family actually end up hurting your family?

5. What role might financial debt play in your marriage decision?

Don't Marry
a "Crude" Dude

Ephesians 4:29

Do not let any unwholesome talk come out of your mouths,
but only what is helpful for building others up according to their
needs, that it may benefit those who listen.

"I remember reading this letter before I was engaged and thinking maybe there were a few changes I needed to make. I definitely
wasn't as "crude" as the "dude" mentioned in the opening of this
chapter, but I was forced to examine my passion and commitment
to holiness and Christ-likeness. As I prepared for engagement and
marriage, I came to realize that one of the things my wife would
need most was a man who loved Jesus and wanted to become more
like Him; this meant I needed to allow Christ to come into all areas
of my life and smooth out some of my rough areas with His grace,
including my tendency toward "crudeness.""

1. Why does our culture seem to enjoy crude or suggestive
   humor?

2. What does Ephesians 4:29 mean practically for relationships? How can you better live according to this Scripture?

3. What are some other areas of "unwholesome talk" besides crudeness?

4. How can "unwholesome talk" be a killer to your marital relationship?

5. Describe a couple that has used communication and humor to build up their relationship rather than tear it down.

One... (No Longer Two)

Matthew 19:5–6

*"... and said, 'For this reason a man will leave his father and mother
and be united to his wife, and the two will become one flesh'?
So they are no longer two, but one. Therefore what God has
joined together, let man not separate."*

"This letter hit home with me due to my past of watching failed relationships due to selfishness of the married couples. Their own self was more important than the marriage. When Dr. Friesen talks about discussions going through the relationship grid, that is something I keep in the back of my head now. How does a man treat situations? Is it for the individual or the whole? It's similar to sports: the collective whole is more important than the individuals."

1. Do you know any married persons who seem to be pursuing their own agenda to the detriment of their marriage? If so, explain.

2. What are some of the "good" things you can see newly married people involved in as individuals that might actually hinder their marriage?

3. How do you think decisions should be made on finances if one spouse brought a large sum of money into the marriage?

4. To what extent do you think you need to receive permission from your spouse before making an independent decision or commitment?

5. Describe a couple you know who are independently gifted but do not seem to act independently from each other.

Does He Have an "Entitlement" Attitude?

Luke 15:11–13

Jesus continued: "There was a man who had two sons. The younger one said to his father, 'Father, give me my share of the estate.' So he divided his property between them. Not long after that, the younger son got together all he had, set off for a distant country and there squandered his wealth in wild living."

"When I was still single, a very wise mentor of mine counseled me by saying, "It takes a great man to be better than none." She explained what a great man would look like and that a servant's heart was one quality I should be on the lookout for. I had observed the character of servant-hearted men on several missions trips, all of whom were already married. I often questioned if a "great man" existed outside of those men already married. When I finally met my husband, I was overwhelmed by how selfless he was and how easily he would lay down his own needs for the needs of others. This letter confirmed that looking at how a man sets aside his needs and desires and serves others says a lot about the condition of his heart."

1. How would you define entitlement? In what ways do you see our culture producing people who live with an entitlement attitude?

2. What are some signals that the person you are dating is entitled?

3. How might entitlement affect your marriage and family?

4. What qualities would be the opposite of entitlement? How can you start developing these qualities in your life?

5. Describe a person or couple who do not act entitled. How do you feel about the way they live?

22

What Kind of Dad Will He Be?

Titus 1:6–9

An elder must be blameless, the husband of but one wife, a man whose children believe and are not open to the charge of being wild and disobedient. Since an overseer is entrusted with God's work, he must be blameless—not overbearing, not quick-tempered, not given to drunkenness, not violent, not pursuing dishonest gain. Rather he must be hospitable, one who loves what is good, who is self-controlled, upright, holy and disciplined. He must hold firmly to the trustworthy message as it has been taught, so that he can encourage others by sound doctrine and refute those who oppose it.

"I have always had a desire to have children and have the opportunity to stay at home and raise them. Therefore, it was really important to me to marry a man whom I knew would want to have children, be a good father to our children, and provide for us in a way that would allow me the opportunity to stay at home to raise our children. When I was dating my future husband, it was important for us to discuss my desire to be a mother and having him support and encourage that desire. Most importantly though, I was blown away by his character and love for God. There is no greater gift I could give our future children than a father who would model a passionate and authentic love for Jesus."

1. Describe your dad in a few sentences. What are some of your great memories? What are some of the memories you would change if you could?

2. When thinking through whom we will marry, why is it critically important to think through what type of father or mother that person will be?

3. What are some of the indicators in a man you may be dating regarding the sort of dad he will likely be? If you are a guy, what kind of dad do you want to be?

4. What are some of the traits you wish to find in the father of your children? If you are a guy, how can you start to develop some of these traits now?

5. Name a dad you really admire. Tell what traits caused him to be the dad you selected. How can our Heavenly Father be another example to us?

Considerations

Convictions

Character

Chemistry

Considerations are those areas that, even though not as founda-
tional as character and convictions, contribute greatly to the ease
and enjoyment of the relationship. These are areas of compatibility. For example, while it is not a moral issue whether or not you
both are passionate about being outdoors, having that preference
in common leads to shared experiences that make marriage much
more enjoyable. Is he fun, spontaneous, and good with people?
Do his lifestyle choices regarding media, music, alcohol, etc., line
up with yours? Are you comfortable with each other whether in
groups or alone? Do you both share enough common interests
to make your life more enjoyable when you're together than when
you're apart?

23

I Hope He Knows
How to Have Fun

John 10:10

"The thief comes only to steal and kill and destroy; I have come that they may have life, and have it to the full."

66 Growing up, I always knew how important it was to find someone with character and convictions. I knew these were important building blocks for a relationship that glorified God. However, I also thought this meant that I would end up with someone who was Godly but ugly, or had great character but wouldn't be fun. It was so refreshing to hear that God not only wants me to end up with a Godly man, but one with whom I can laugh and enjoy life. I want to have a relationship where life is experienced to the full! 99

1. How would you evaluate the "fun quotient" of the family in which you were raised?

2. How is "fun" presently expressed in your dating relationship, if you are dating? Why is having fun important?

3. What would a healthy "fun" dating relationship look like to you?

4. If this is an area of challenge for you, how do you think you could include more fun in your relationship?

5. Name a fun couple in your life. What makes them fun? How would you like to be like them?

Frankly, I'm Crazy Enough Without the Bottle

Ephesians 5:18

Do not get drunk on wine, which leads to debauchery. Instead, be filled with the Spirit.

"I was raised in a home where alcohol was not a part of my growing-up experience. Neither of my parents chose to drink, and from an early age in life I have held on to that conviction as one of my own. One of my best friends in high school was the victim of a date rape involving alcohol and that was enough for me to stay away. As I have gotten older and have passed the legal drinking age, I have continued to hold that conviction. I respect a guy who can socialize without alcohol and who has enough personality to engage other people without the added confidence of a shot. Most importantly, I have felt safe in relationships knowing that we are both operating under our own control, without fear that we will wake up the next morning wondering what happened."

1. What role has alcohol played in your family of origin?

2. What has been your experience or observations regarding the benefits or drawbacks of alcohol during the dating period of one's life?

3. What might be some of the negatives in a relationship if one partner is comfortable with drinking and the other is not?

4. What is your position on alcohol in your relationship? How important is it that your future mate share your convictions on this matter?

5. Have you seen any marriages affected by the use of alcohol? What have you observed?

Do You Both Have Similar Passions?

Philippians 2:1–2

If you have any encouragement from being united with Christ, if any comfort from his love, if any fellowship with the Spirit, if any tenderness and compassion, then make my joy complete by being like-minded, having the same love, being one in spirit and purpose.

Without knowing it, I've lived most of my life thinking that having Jesus in common was enough. Pop culture talks about how opposites attract, and I've witnessed so many Christian friends get into relationships with other Christians for two reasons: common faith and physical attraction. Actually, this is how I thought as well. After a relationship with a great Christian guy who I thought was really cute, I become a firm believer that a couple needs to have many common interests outside a mutual faith. After the infatuation wore off, I wanted to enjoy doing the same things together or have long conversations about a topic that interested us both. I thought about my parents, who have been married for 30 years, driving to visit me in college. What did they talk about for the 5-hour drive? Would I be able to spend a lifetime with a person who doesn't like things like independent movies, going to the ballet, politics, or talking about ideas? Maybe, but the marriage would probably be harder work. I decided I couldn't handle it, and I am now enjoying how important common interests are in another relationship.

1. What are your greatest passions in life?

2. If you are in a dating relationship, what would you say the other's passions are?

3. How do you discern what each other's passions are and their compatibility before marriage?

4. What might be some dangers if you don't share your deepest passions with your spouse? How might that be different before or after marriage?

5. Have you seen couples whose passions are very different? How have they made it work? What have you observed about couples who both share the same passions?

How Important Are Common Interests?

Genesis 29:16–18

Now Laban had two daughters; the name of the older was Leah, and the name of the younger was Rachel. Leah had weak eyes, but Rachel was lovely in form, and beautiful. Jacob was in love with Rachel and said, "I'll work for you seven years in return for your younger daughter Rachel."

I am an active person who has always had a number of hobbies and interests. When I was dating my husband, he wanted to share in all the things I enjoyed and told me how it had expanded him as a person. He had said before we dated that his demanding job had kept him from doing all the things I liked to do. Unfortunately, after the marriage, he stopped participating in these activities and we had little in common. It would have been helpful if I had taken a picture of who he was when I met him vs. who he tried to become to please me during dating.

1. How and where do you like to spend a free weekend?

2. How important do you think it is that you and your mate have the exact same answer?

3. Do you think a couple can grow to have the same interests over time? What is the danger of hoping that your significant other will end up having interests similar to yours?

4. What do you see as the biggest dangers for couples that have very different interests from each other?

5. Describe a couple, if you know one, whose interests are polar opposites. What effect has it had on their marriage? Describe a couple that seems to share the same basic interests. How has that affected their marriage?

Who Are
Your Counselors?

Proverbs 15:22

Plans fail for lack of counsel, but with many advisers they succeed.

"It was only after the fact that I was able to recognize the visible signs that the marriage I had just entered was doomed for divorce court. I wish I had read this letter despite my rush to get going with the plans we were making to be married. I wish I had not gone so fast that the people who would normally be considered wise counsel to me were not even involved until they received the wedding invitation. I could have avoided so much heartache and pain had I only heeded the advice in this letter and given it the time and counsel required to determine that this marriage would fall apart from the moment it began. The writing was on the wall, but I refused to read it."

1. Name your three closest advisors when it comes to relationship issues. If you don't have any, how can you be more proactive in finding a wise advisor?

2. What is it about each of them that make you want to listen to their advice? Do they share your values and faith position?

3. Have you ever been the "advisor" to someone and found that for some reason they don't come to you for advice on a relationship? Why is humility important when it comes to seeking out Godly advice?

4. What could you envision that might cause you to move ahead in a relationship against the advice of family and friends?

5. What do you think should be the qualities of your "relationship advisors"? How much stock would you put in their advice regarding your relationships? Explain.

Do You Like Him in Public?

Song of Solomon 2:3

Like an apple tree among the trees of the forest
is my lover among the young men.
I delight to sit in his shade, and his fruit is sweet to my taste.

"I remember reading this letter for the first time and feeling like this was something I really needed to wrestle with. I had always been attracted to guys who were "the life of the party" and very outgoing in public settings. However, when I was dating my soon-to-be-husband, I quickly realized that he was not the life of the party. He was not awkward in public settings by any means, but he was not "the loud guy," and preferred to connect with a few people rather than with everyone in the room. At first this bothered me, but the longer we dated the more I realized how much I loved the unique way God designed him to be, and I was very at ease with him in public."

1. The author writes, "I want you to consider the fact that enjoying a relationship in private is one thing, while enjoying a relationship in the public arena is a different story" (p. 123). How can a relationship be different in private than it is in public?

2. What can be some of the challenges for a couple that thrives only in private?

3. Why is it important that you not feel constantly apologetic for your partner in public?

4. If you really like someone who is simply awkward in public, what might you do?

5. Do you know any couples that fit the examples of this letter? How have you seen it affect them? How do couples who are comfortable with each other's behavior in public settings have an advantage in their relationship?

29

Do You Like Being Alone Together?

Proverbs 18:24

A man of many companions may come to ruin,
but there is a friend who sticks closer than a brother.

"Everyone said what a perfect couple we would make. He seemed so comfortable in front of people. He was engaging, fun, and easy to be around. What I was not expecting was that when we were alone, there was complete silence unless I initiated and kept the conversation going. I felt like the babbling brook speaking to the Dead Sea. He seemed to listen well because he never talked, but I became tired of feeling pressured to lead the conversations, and eventually tired of the relationship. I don't need someone who talks my ear off, but I do want someone genuinely interested in me and willing to talk with me, even in private."

1. Have you ever known a couple that seems to be "on" when they are in public or on stage, but later you find their marriage is falling apart behind the scenes? If so, what were your thoughts and observations about this?

2. What would be some concerns if your relationship were more "successful" when you were with others than when you were alone together?

3. What would likely take place if you and your boyfriend were asked to spend four hours together—but you could not watch TV, listen to music, be with anyone else, or be physically involved?

4. Does the experiment mentioned above sound like an enjoyable night? What would be some of your concerns if it doesn't?

5. Describe a couple you admire that seems to be equally at ease in private and in public.

*C*hemistry

Convictions
Character
Considerations

Although "chemistry" is often the first thing that catches our attention or attracts us to someone, it seldom sustains the relationship.

Chemistry may not sustain the relationship, but it sure makes it more fun. It was God's idea to make us sexual beings and to have this be such a strong and enjoyable part of our relationship. It is designed for married couples to experience most fully in coming together emotionally and physically in sexual intercourse. The Bible speaks of it being intoxicating, and it is. God designed us to be "out of our minds" while making love. Within marriage, it is a wonderful gift that allows us to forget life's stresses and routines and just revel in each other. Outside of marriage, it also is intoxicating and we become "out of our minds"—not a good state to be in while making the second most important decision of your life. Sexual involvement "feels" like intimacy, but is not necessarily.

Two questions to ask yourself about chemistry: Do you have it? and, Do you control it? Don't walk down the aisle without it and don't walk down the aisle until you can control it. You should be fighting to not compromise in this area. As you become more and more committed to each other, you should feel a strong desire to experience oneness physically.

Do you control it? If you do not control your sexual drives before marriage and honor God in this area, you are essentially saying your hormones are more important than scripture. Make sure you are marrying someone who holds scripture above his or her hormonal desires.

Chemistry is a wonderful gift from God in marriage, but used apart from His instructions, it can easily cause explosions that are damaging—and sometimes fatal—to a relationship.

Marital Chemistry 101

Song of Solomon 4:1

How beautiful you are, my darling! Oh, how beautiful!
Your eyes behind your veil are doves.
Your hair is like a flock of goats descending from Mount Gilead.

"My wife is hot! Thank God this letter reminded me that it is totally appropriate to wait for God to send you someone to whom you are physically attracted. But this letter also reminds us that physical attraction is never enough. Beyond my wife's "hotness," she is someone who loves God, loves God's word, and loves God's people. As I think about my wife, I think about how good God is and how He loves giving good gifts to His children. If you're single, be patient and wait for God's best. He is willing to "blow you away" by blessing you with someone beyond your imagination. "

1. How do you think your list and God's list of the top characteristics and attributes of a Godly husband or wife would be similar? How would they be different?

2. How have your parents taught you about the wife or husband you should marry?

3. What is wrong with marrying someone with character, even if they don't do anything for you from a chemistry standpoint? Why is chemistry important?

4. Why would God care about giving us someone who meets our needs and desires in every way? What does this teach us about God?

5. Now, on that list of yours, what are the top "non-negotiable" traits in the person you want to marry? What about the strongly desired and the bonus attributes? Which of these are worth holding out for? Which ones do you think God cares about?

Male/Female Differences and Sexuality

Genesis 1:27

So God created man in his own image,
in the image of God he created him;
male and female he created them.

Genesis 2:18

The Lord God said, "It is not good for the man to be alone.
I will make a helper suitable for him."

"Different." Now that is an understatement. I have struggled for many years with understanding what different yet equal really meant. My interpretation of "help" was always to be "not good enough to be the real thing." I now understand that to "help" is to be something to someone that they cannot be for themselves. My husband needs me to be the "wife" to his being "husband." In the area of being different sexually, it is critical that we understand that men and women are wired differently. Even more important is for us to understand not only how oneself is wired, but to understand how the other is wired.

1. In what ways do you see our culture involved in gender neutralization? What impact does this have on the Christian community?

2. What do you see as the major differences between male and female? How is this a part of God's design?

3. What do you think about the author's observations about male and female wiring when it comes to sexual relationships?

4. Do you have any examples where you felt some expectations of physical involvement at the end of the date? What is the best way to honor God with physical involvement within a dating relationship?

5. Describe someone of the opposite sex who has honored you and cared for you relationally without expecting any physical payback.

You Asked
about Modesty

1 Peter 3:3–4

Your beauty should not come from outward adornment, such as braided hair and the wearing of gold jewelry and fine clothes. Instead, it should be that of your inner self, the unfading beauty of a gentle and quiet spirit, which is of great worth in God's sight.

"Modesty was a hot topic in our family and one that was difficult to fully understand. I always struggled that being modest was synonymous with being weird. The switch came when I heard young men discussing what girls' clothes (or lack of clothes) did to them. The guys challenged me as a sister to wear clothes that allowed guys I interacted with to see Christ in me, not just my body. I realized that that was my desire for the man I married: I wanted a man who desired purity, and I wanted to help with that cause. Although it was good to hear, I still believed in the back of my head that you won't really get a guy's attention unless you dress a certain way. This thought was turned upside down when I lived in Africa. I had to wear super modest clothes (culturally) and was in scrubs 95% of the time. I never would have thought I would have caught someone's eye. However, it was in this humbled state that I met the man of my dreams. Honestly, it was refreshing. I knew that he must love *who* I am to fall for me in this state! What a safe feeling that was; I was confident it could only go up from there. God reminded me that beauty truly is His making, not our own. We often tarnish what He has made by trying to impress on our own accord; however, He is the master artist—allow Him to display His beauty through you."

1. By whom and how do you think fashion trends are determined?

2. Why do you think some women dress immodestly? How do you feel about it?

3. What are some of the problems with attracting a man with your body?

4. How could Christian guys be more helpful to you in the area of modesty? Have you ever talked to a Christian brother about this?

5. List some specific guidelines that might be used in defining modesty.

Only Big Lures Catch Prize "Fish"

Psalm 1:1–2

Blessed is the man who does not walk in the counsel of the wicked
or stand in the way of sinners or sit in the seat of mockers.
But his delight is in the law of the Lord,
and on his law he meditates day and night.

"I felt as if someone hit me over the head when I read this. I have been struggling lately with the fact that there aren't men (the type of Godly man I'm looking for) around me. I often find myself at home while other girls at school seem to always be out with their new love. I think this was such a great metaphor about the types of men you are looking for and what "lures" self select the type of men you will find. The expectation and standards you set for yourself may limit options, but they weed out the "smaller" "weaker" fish you don't want anyways. I re-read this chapter when I get discouraged about being single—and remember what Mama Friesen once said, "It's better to be alone than to be married to the wrong person."

1. What do you feel is the primary motivation to date?

2. Practically speaking, what does a "little lure" fisherman/woman look like?

3. In what ways does a "big lure" fisherman/woman differ?

4. Do you agree with the author that the "lure" you use will determine what kind of person you will attract?

5. Talk about some "big lure" men and women you know and what their lives look like. How do you feel about their decisions about how to live life?

Where You "Fish" Does Affect Your "Catch"

Luke 5:4–6

When he had finished speaking, he said to Simon,
"Put out into deep water, and let down the nets for a catch."
Simon answered, "Master, we've worked hard all night and haven't
caught anything. But because you say so, I will let down the nets."
When they had done so, they caught such a large number of fish
that their nets began to break.

"I have been fishing many times and am sad to say, I have caught the wrong fish. Some were caught because of their beauty; others were caught because they had lots of scales ($$). Whatever the reasons why they were caught, here's the main flop: I was always in the ponds when I should have been in the oceans. Walking faithfully with the Lord for about 3 years, I truly understand the content of this letter and that it makes sense. The only way to find the right kind of man is by being in the areas Godly men hang out. Prize fish swim in the deep waters, not shallow. Godly men "swim" in places of worship and service, not in clubs and places of self-indulgence."

1. What are some of the "shallow" water areas most appealing to young people today?

2. If a person were interested in a "game fish," what would motivate him or her to fish in the "shallows?"

3. What would you describe as "deep water" areas today?

4. What are some ways that might help you discern if a fish swimming in the "deep water" is not a game fish at all?

5. How would God want you to pursue someone in a faithful and God-honoring way?

Take a Look
Before Taking the Hook

Luke 8:17

"For there is nothing hidden that will not be disclosed, and nothing concealed that will not be known or brought out into the open."

"Growing up, I was taught that in order to be loved, I needed to earn it. It never occurred to me that I had a choice in a relationship with a man so that I could actually say *no* to something he was asking for. As a result, I felt an obligation to go along with men even when what they were asking of me was something I should be preserving for marriage. This letter helped me see that being asked to take part in physical involvement before marriage is a clear indication of the character of the man and his lack of commitment to God—even if I met him in a church group and he knows all the right things to say, the Bible stories, etc. It shows that he is at best weak in his faith and at worst an impostor."

1. Have you ever fallen for someone only to find they looked worse instead of better the more you got to know them? If so, explain.

2. How does "play with the bait" translate into the dating scene?

3. Regarding the scenarios mentioned that might entice someone to swallow too soon, which do you think you could be most susceptible to? How is this different for men and women?

4. What if you did take the bait too quickly? What hope is there?

5. What specific actions can protect you in the future from swallowing the bait too soon?

What Does God Think about Sex?

Genesis 2:25

The man and his wife were both naked, and they felt no shame.

“Well, I don't know if the author's rap skills are up to par, but in this chapter he gives his readers some great theology. The Christian community is filled with people who want young people to remain sexually pure until marriage. Obviously, their efforts come from the truth found in Scripture; however, often times their message seems to be couched with negative overtones and we miss out on learning about God's glorious design for sex. This letter reminds us that sex is an amazing gift that God has blessed us with to enjoy within His boundaries. I pray that more and more people will appreciate God's great gift of sex and do everything possible to experience it only within the greater gift of marriage. ”

1. Where have you received most of your instruction regarding sexuality?

2. What has been your view of what God thinks about sex? Where has this view come from?

3. Why is it important to believe that marital sexual expression is one of God's great ideas? What are practical ways we can develop a Biblical perspective on sex?

4. How would you describe what your non-believer friends think about Christians and sex?

5. Why is it sometimes hard to believe that God really has our best interests in mind regarding our sexuality?

Don't Awaken Love Until Its Time

Song of Solomon 2:7

Daughters of Jerusalem, I charge you by the gazelles and by the does of the field: Do not arouse or awaken love until it so desires.

"I've always thought of myself as a disciplined man when it comes to physical relationships and temptations. I remained a virgin until I married in my late 30's. Surely I had mastered this part of a disciplined life. However, it wasn't until after I read this letter that I fully understood the reasons behind the wisdom and commands to keep ourselves pure and not to awaken love until its proper time. There are clear, irrefutable barriers to protect us from opening our hearts, thoughts, and physical passions too early in the relationship. We are often tempted to push the boundaries, but just as a banana peeled and then left open for too long begins to spoil, so does the freshness of our physical desire for each other if entered into too early."

1. Why do you think Solomon's wife admonishes her sisters not to awaken love until its time? Is this applicable to both men and women?

2. Using the banana illustration, in what ways might love not ripen if "opened" prematurely?

3. How might you view God's guidelines for sexual purity as a protection rather than a limitation?

4. How have you seen in your friends' lives "love gone rotten" when they have experienced a sexual relationship prematurely? Have you seen "love gone rotten" in your own life?

5. Describe a couple that has not "peeled the banana" until their wedding night. How do you see this as a benefit to their relationship?

What Constitutes Sexual Purity?

1 Timothy 5:2

[Treat] . . . older women as mothers, and younger women as sisters, with absolute purity.

"I was talking to a student who had already been sexually active. She was asking me why it wasn't okay to do everything sexually with each other as long as they didn't have sex. I took a dollar out of my purse and tore little pieces off. Even though they were all little pieces, at the end, when I was done, there was only a small piece of the dollar left. Then I said, "this is what you have to offer to your husband on your wedding night when you mess around with guys you *may* marry."

There are men who respect this, and there are men who don't. That's the ugly truth. Set the bar for these men and yourself and a Godly man will want the same thing. Wait for that guy. It's worth it. You're worth it."

1. Why is sexual involvement for most couples an "expectation" if they have been dating for a while?

2. How do you think it would affect couples if they adopted the "don't sexually stimulate one another before marriage" policy?

3. What "harm" is there in being sexually involved as long as you don't have intercourse? How have you seen premarital sexual involvement impact others or even yourself?

4. What are some ways couples could express their "love" for each other if they refrained from sexual involvement?

5. Do you know any couples that have refrained from expressing themselves sexually to each other? How does this impact their relationship?

Four Scriptural Guidelines for Physical Involvement

1 Corinthians 13:4

Love is patient, love is kind.
It does not envy, it does not boast, it is not proud.

"During dating, I violated every guideline that this chapter teaches. I was left empty, broken, and far from God at the end of each relationship. When I met the man who is now my husband, I looked to God for wisdom, and through Godly mentors, I was shown God's plan for physical involvement. While we were dating, we wanted to go as slow as we could physically. I felt so loved and special because I wasn't seen as an object or lusted after. I knew he was with me because he loved me and respected me. The love and respect we showed one another during dating has carried over into our marriage and is continuing to grow."

1. How do you think most couples determine their guidelines for sexual involvement prior to marriage? How can you become more intentional in setting God-honoring guidelines for sexual involvement?

2. Why do you think so many Christian couples have sex before marriage even though scripture is clear that such involvement is sin?

3. In what ways do you think premature sexual involvement could be seen as a form of selfishness?

4. How would you practically define "treat each other in all purity"?

5. How do you think a couple is able to determine if they are "lusting" after each other?

Four Practical Guidelines for Physical Involvement

1 Thessalonians 4:3–5

It is God's will that you should be sanctified: that you should avoid sexual immorality; that each of you should learn to control his own body in a way that is holy and honorable, not in passionate lust like the heathen, who do not know God.

“Agreeing to limits on physical intimacy during a dating relationship is a wise idea. These four rules are simple, easy to remember, and keys to a godly and enjoyable relationship. It is true that people are turned on in different ways, so these four guidelines don't eradicate all temptation. However, I'm not for living on the edge when it may hinder my seeking God's best in my relationship. I say, until it's time to go all the way, follow these rules to avoid greater temptation and sin.”

1. Discuss the first rule, "Four on the floor." Is it helpful? Is it achievable? How can you implement it?

2. Discuss the second rule, "Hands off." Is it helpful? Is it achievable? How can you implement it?

3. Discuss the third rule, "Clothes on." Is it helpful? Is it achievable? How can you implement it?

4. Discuss the fourth rule, "Tongue in." Is it helpful? Is it achievable? How can you implement it?

5. What would a dating relationship look like if you followed these guidelines? Would you like to be in such a relationship? What is preventing you?

The Fallacy of Parallel Physical Involvement

Ecclesiastes 3:1,5b

There is a time for everything, and a season for every activity under heaven . . . a time to embrace and a time to refrain . . .

"The world taught me that sexual compatibility is the top priority in a relationship and that gender equality is the desired state to achieve. This left me constantly needing to maintain my sexual desirability, which pushed me towards believing I was only an object for sex in the eyes of men. Gender equality left me feeling inadequate, being compared to a man, and socially pressured into letting go of any sense of womanhood. Christ is renewing my mind to see sex as having been designed for an emotional and spiritual relationship in a marriage. This has created in me a strong value to wait to experience it then, and also to see a man with the unique characteristic of a leader who encourages me to submit in a way that is not demeaning, yet brings a sense of peace and restoration."

1. What do you think most Christians would deem "appropriate" sexual involvement on the first date; after a week of dating; after a month of dating; after 3 months of dating; after 6 months of dating; after a year of dating; after engagement; one night before the wedding? How are these "appropriate" levels determined?

2. What do you see as the pluses and minuses of the "parallel" thinking approach?

3. Discuss the position of concern about "sexual compatibility" if you have not been sexually involved before marriage?

4. Why might it be that a couple could seem "sexually compatible" before marriage and yet struggle with their sexual life after marriage?

5. What would you like your honeymoon to be like sexually? What do you think might contribute to it being your dream come true?

Sexual Stimulation
Is for Marriage

Ephesians 5:3

*But among you there must not be even a hint of sexual immorality,
or of any kind of impurity, or of greed,
because these are improper for God's holy people.*

"In my junior year of high school, I began dating a guy who loved God, was a leader, was respectful, and had the same desire as I did to remain pure until marriage. He treated me respectfully, but like any couples we were tempted sexually. My boyfriend had an older mentor who suggested that we make a "relationship contract" outlining our goals for our relationship. We included things like remaining sexually pure, reading our Bible, etc. We signed them and kept them in our Bibles as a constant reminder. We didn't rely solely on accountability from each other, but also from my youth pastor that we knew well. We made a list of questions for him to call and ask us. After 6 years, by the grace of God, we made it to our wedding day and were able to give each other the best gift of all. I had no doubt when I said "I do" that I would be cherished and led because he had been treating me that way the entire relationship! Don't lower your standards. God wants the best for you—that's why He's outlined His plan for us. "

1. What strikes you about the "armpit" story?

2. What could be wrong with a little sexual stimulation before marriage?

3. Who should set the standards for physical involvement regarding sexual stimulation? Why?

4. What are some of the safeguards we might take to make sure not even a "hint of sexual immorality" is found within us?

5. Describe a person, without naming him or her, that you feel has been intentional about staying away from sexual immorality. How do think this person does it?

43

Your Mom Says It's the Best Gift I Gave Her

Hebrews 11:24–25

By faith Moses, when he had grown up, refused to be known as the son of Pharaoh's daughter. He chose to be mistreated along with the people of God rather than to enjoy the pleasures of sin for a short time.

" I've spent a lot of time with women who believe that if they don't "give it up" for a guy, they'll be dateless. I challenge them to believe that if a guy isn't really interested in being with them because of who they are and not because of how they feel, he doesn't deserve them. Every woman needs to know that she will be cherished and not just handled. I am humbled to have had a man who led our dating relationship with Christlikeness, a key characteristic of which is unselfishness. He elevated my own sense of value by protecting our relationship from being driven by hormones. I was never left to wonder if he only hung with me because of what he could get. I could see first hand that he was more committed to honoring the Lord and me than in getting his healthy sexual drive temporarily satisfied. It was clear to me that his character was expressed in his daily choices, which allowed our relationship to develop in the context of purity and Christlikeness. Because physical involvement contributes a huge distortion factor to a dating relationship, effectively skewing objectivity, it makes it harder to make a good life-long decision. I felt more confident that we were making the right decision to get married because we had reduced the distortion factor significantly by not acting on our strong physical attraction for one another. As I reflect on my life, I'd be hard pressed to come up with anything else that has made me feel more loved and valued than having been so honored by him during our courtship. "

1. What are some indications from our culture that sex is not the glue that holds relationships together?

2. If sex before marriage is wrong, why does it feel so good?

3. What do you think of the letter from the girl at camp? What do you think about her boyfriend?

4. How do you feel about the author's decision not to kiss before his engagement?

5. How could premature physical involvement hinder you from truly getting to know your boyfriend or girlfriend?

Emotional Hooks
in Relationships

Proverbs 4:23

Above all else, guard your heart, for it is the wellspring of life.

66 I was taught how important emotional boundaries are in relationships, but always found it difficult to know how to make them and, frankly, why they were they so important anyway. It seemed hard enough to keep physically pure. This chapter helped me see how easy it is to get "hooked" emotionally, just as it is physically. Saying things like "I'll always love you" or "You're the only one for me" are the emotional equivalents of making out. It makes objective thinking very difficult. I know how to guard my heart, which has helped as I am navigating the confusing channels of dating. 99

1. Do you know people who have returned to unhealthy relationships? Why would we go back to what we know is harmful and destructive?

2. We have been pretty clear on defining sexual fornication. Is emotional fornication possible, and if so, how would you define it?

3. Do you know any situations where the couple have been very careful in their physical expression of love, but have been heavily involved emotionally? What does it look like and how can it be harmful?

4. Do you feel it is possible to "pace" a relationship? If so, what are practical ways you can you slow it down?

5. How can premature promises to a person hinder your ability to really get to know them?

45

How Do I Know If He Has Truly Changed?

2 Corinthians 5:17

Therefore, if anyone is in Christ, he is a new creation;
the old has gone, the new has come!

"I am so grateful to serve and know a God who transforms us in real and practical ways. I certainly have changed for the better over the years as I've pursued Christ, and I know it is essential when loving others to believe that we can truly change by God's power, too. But it is also important to establish safeguards in our lives to be able to discern with clear eyes whether the change needed in our boyfriend or girlfriend's life has really occurred. Love and infatuation can sometimes hinder us from detecting true, deep, and lasting change in someone's life. For me, I try to establish very open communication with close friends so they can help me distinguish true change in my romantic interest's life, or if I am making excuses in order to be in a relationship. This takes a lot of humility, but it's worth it!"

1. Without using names, describe someone you know who seemed to change for his or her significant other, but eventually went back to former ways.

2. List some ways you can help ensure that you will continue to mature in your love for Christ while in a relationship with someone. Why is it that our relationship with Jesus often gets sidelined while we are pursuing a romantic relationship?

3. From your experience, what is it that causes couples to break up and then return to each other?

4. What are some of the ways you can determine if another person's change is genuine or not?

5. Describe someone you know who genuinely underwent a change of character, values, or convictions. How did that affect this person's relationships?

46

How Do You Know the "Real Deal"?

Colossians 2:10

*. . . and you have been given fullness in Christ,
who is the head over every power and authority.*

"I met him at college. He was a star football player, fun, handsome, and intelligent. We immediately hit it off and before long were in a fairly serious dating relationship. As we grew deeper in our relationship I shared with him my faith position and how important it was to me. Eventually I told him I could not continue our relationship unless he became a Christian. I was elated when he started coming regularly to church with me. Before long he said he believed. Finally, I felt that the last barrier to our heading toward marriage had been eradicated. It was not until I met with my mentor that I questioned the genuineness of his profession at all. My mentor only asked me one question. When you are away on a Sunday, does he attend church on his own? That started me noticing that he didn't want to be in a men's group, didn't want to attend anything at church unless I was there, and didn't want to hang out with Christians unless they were my friends. We eventually broke up and he has not entered a church since. I was flattered that he wanted to follow Christ for me, but that is not an acceptable motivation for coming to Christ."

1. What are the areas of compatibility that you desire in a romantic relationship that are non-negotiable for you?

2. What do you feel are the best ways to see if these areas of compatibility are genuine?

3. How do you know if the moral positions of your friend are genuine, or if he is simply adopting your positions so he can be in a romantic relationship with you?

4. In what area do you feel you are most vulnerable to adapting in order to have a romantic relationship with someone?

5. What do you believe it is in a person that prepares them to be less vulnerable to shifting values for others?

Marriage by Choice, Not Obligation

John 15:16–17

You did not choose me, but I chose you and appointed you to go and bear fruit—fruit that will last. Then the Father will give you whatever you ask in my name. This is my command: Love each other.

" I am embarrassed to say this, but after 22 years of marriage I still have a nagging doubt as to whether my husband would have asked me to marry him *if* I were not pregnant with our child. Our parents pretty much said we needed to marry each other, and we did. But the nagging, usually unspoken, question that comes up every time we are in a bad place is would we have chosen each other? Being chosen really is special. I wish for you, as you enter marriage, to have that security that I never had, and most likely never will. "

1. Have you ever done something wrong and tried to "make it right" by doing something else that ended up making things worse? Explain.

2. Why might people in the Christian community be more inclined to "make things right" by marrying the person they have been sexually active with or have become pregnant with?

3. Why might it not necessarily be the best to marry someone you have been sexually active with or have become pregnant with?

4. Why is being chosen rather than being "forced" to get married such a big deal?

5. How would you advise a friend of yours who is pregnant and trying to decide whether or not to marry the father of her child?

It's Never Too Late to Do the Right Thing

1 Peter 1:23

For you have been born again, not of perishable seed, but of imperishable, through the living and enduring word of God.

"Obviously, making Godly choices from the start is the best! I certainly found myself in a situation in which I/we had not made decisions with God's design and best in mind. We had instant gratification and worldliness at the forefront of our minds. We thought we needed to find out if we were "compatible" in every way before marriage, so we lived together. Thankfully, someone who was invested not only in God's design for marriage, but also in us, "called us out." We made some difficult decisions and changes that profoundly affected our relationship as a pre-married couple. We moved into separate living situations and became sexually celibate. Now, as a married couple, God's grace and love have washed us clean! It is never too late to start doing the right thing!"

1. What does the story of the couple in letter 48 illustrate about God's love for us?

2. How have you seen God's forgiveness expressed in your life?

3. Do you live as if you have truly been forgiven by God from all your past sins? What is keeping you from experiencing the freedom that comes with faith in Christ's life, death, and resurrection?

4. How have you seen God's forgiveness and "second start" positively affect a couple you know? What practical steps could you take to receive a "second start?"

5. How does hearing stories like these affect your relationships and your motivation toward obedience?

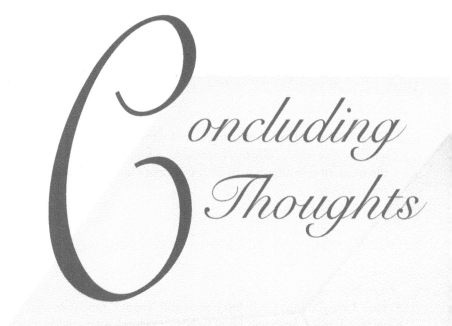

Concluding Thoughts

At this point, you may have lists made, pros and cons, and hopefully a more objective view of God's design for lasting and vital relationships. At the end of the day, you are the one who will live with your mate for life. No matter what your friends, parents, and pastor say, *you* are the one who is making a covenant vow for life, as my wife, Virginia, told our girls countless times. Before marriage, you are able to decide whom it is you will submit to and respect the rest of your life, but after marriage the decision has been made. *You* alone will walk down the aisle. If you are alone in being positive that he is the one for you, while significant others have strong reservations, think carefully before taking that final step.

Most of all, I wish for you to have a man who will walk with the Lord faithfully and care for you sacrificially all the days of your life, and that you will enjoy all that God designed marriage to be.

Men, be such a man, and hold out for a woman who is fully committed to glorifying God in every area of her life.

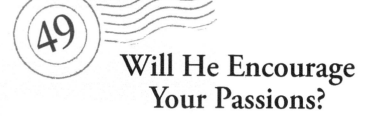

Will He Encourage Your Passions?

Philippians 2:3–4

Do nothing out of selfish ambition or vain conceit, but in humility consider others better than yourselves. Each of you should look not only to your own interests, but also to the interests of others.

"Although my wife and I share very similar passions, our occupations and geographical locations kept us apart for nearly two years while dating. At the time, the easiest thing to do would have been to drop everything and figure out how to just be together. Alternatively, we could have easily, but sadly, walked away from each other and pursued our individual dreams and goals. What kept us in it was not only the acknowledgement and realization that we were God's best for each other, but that our long-term passions, which we shared, would only be realized with patience and waiting upon His timing. The questions posited to his daughters in this letter drove straight to the crux of our dilemma: Are we better off walking away from each other or walking away from our current goals and dreams? For me, it was simple. My wife is God's best for me, and however hard it's been at times to remain patient, we both know we encourage each other in this specific way that no one else can."

1. How can you practically and creatively be someone who encourages the passions of your spouse?

2. How do you feel couples should deal with their relationship if it seems their passions don't co-exist well?

3. How would you feel if the person you were planning to marry said he/she would not follow you wherever your job took you?

4. Do you know any couples that really seem to have different individual passions, but appear to work well as a couple?

5. Ideally, how would you like your marriage to look in the area of passions?

This Decision Will Affect the Rest of Your Life!

Ephesians 5:33

However, each one of you also must love his wife as he loves himself, and the wife must respect her husband.

"We met and had our first date on New Years Eve 1955. I think we were immediately attracted to each other and we both felt like this could very well be the person God has for me as a "life partner." Eight months later we knew we were ready to make a life commitment. We announced our engagement and ten months later we were married. God has been so good. We are better together and have not had a perfect marriage by any means, but are still each other's best friends. Marrying each other was the best decision we have ever made, next to accepting Christ into our lives. God has given us two sons and nine grandchildren. We have enjoyed individual careers and joint ministry beyond our greatest imaginations. This year we will be married 55 years. We still love God and each other with our whole heart and now know more fully than ever how important this decision really was!"

1. As you read the seven pieces of "advice," comment on or discuss each one and the level of importance you would say it should have for your dating or marital relationship.

- Go slow:

- Vital Christian:

- Sexual purity:

- Good provider:

- Man you will respect/woman you will love:

- Approval from trusted family and friends:

- Potential as a father/mother:

2. What other principles would you propose if you were giving the advice?

Then Who Will Ever Get Married, Dad?

Luke 6:47–49

"I will show you what he is like who comes to me and hears my words and puts them into practice. He is like a man building a house, who dug down deep and laid the foundation on rock. When a flood came, the torrent struck that house but could not shake it, because it was well built. But the one who hears my words and does not put them into practice is like a man who built a house on the ground without a foundation. The moment the torrent struck that house, it collapsed and its destruction was complete."

When I was in my early 20's, I met with my mentor/pastor and the subject of guys came up. I had just ended a relationship in which I had made some serious compromises. During this meeting he challenged me to make a list of the qualities and characteristics of my dream husband. The list was to include non-negotiable character qualities and some "preferences." I made that list and put it in my Bible. It was a constant reminder to me that God had a man for me who would be more than I could even imagine if I would just wait for His best. My list:

- has a vital walk with God
- has a passion for ministry
- understands and supports my passions
- loves my family
- is someone I can laugh with
- is musically gifted
- will lead me and our future family
- cherishes me
- is someone I would respect with all my heart
- is good looking ☺

I showed my husband the list the morning after our wedding and explained to him that he was an answer to my prayers and the greatest gift God had ever given me. We laughed together because my husband is not musically gifted, but we still thought it was pretty amazing how faithful God is.

"

1. If you were to list, in order, what most relationships today are built on in our culture, consider these categories: Convictions, Character, Considerations, Chemistry. How would you rank each one and why?

2. What order do you feel is most beneficial?

3. Describe what you have seen or experienced in relationships where your proposed order was not kept.

4. Describe a relationship that was, from your observation, built on Convictions first, followed by Character, then Considerations, and lastly, but still essential, Chemistry.

5. Which out of these four is the greatest challenge for you to keep in order? Explain.

Finishing Together

Matthew 25:21

"His master replied, 'Well done, good and faithful servant!
You have been faithful with a few things; I will put you in charge
of many things. Come and share your master's happiness!'"

"Author Gary Thomas says that claiming you have a difficult marriage is redundant, because *every* marriage is difficult. Staying married and finishing together is a result of character and the disciplines of love developed over the years, rather than the immediate emotions of love, which can change so quickly. Many people quit hiking when it gets personally hard, without thinking what quitting might mean to the others with whom they are hiking. When we quit hiking because of the difficulty of the trail, we miss the incredible vistas that await us at the top of the mountain. So it is with marriage. Marry someone with whom you can keep hiking, and look forward to enjoying mountaintop vistas together."

1. What is it that strikes you in this letter?

2. What similarities or differences do you imagine your own father would write you about in a series of letters regarding your future decisions?

3. What are some of the main truths you are taking away from this series of letters?

4. How have these letters affected your ideas about who you might marry some day?

5. Whom do you know that can help you be more objective about the relationships you are involved in?

6. Take a few minutes to pray:

   • That God would lead you to a woman or man who will honor you and honor God.

   • That you as a couple would do everything possible to honor God by following His design for relationships, sexual involvement, and marriage.

   • That you and your future spouse would finish together for the glory of God.

8-week Discussion Guide

5

From Letter 40. Discuss the "Four Practical Guidelines for Physical Involvement." Are they helpful? Are they achievable? How can you implement them?

From Letter 41. Why might it be that a couple could seem "sexually compatible" before marriage and yet struggle with their sexual life after marriage?

Week 7: Chemistry (continued)
Letters 42–48

From Letter 42. What are some of the safeguards we might take to make sure "not a hint of sexual immorality" is found within us?

From Letter 43. What are some of the ways you can show your love for another, other than through physical involvement?

From Letter 44. Do you know any situations where the couple have been very careful in their physical expression of love, but have been heavily involved emotionally? What does that look like?

From Letter 45. What are some of the ways you can determine if another person's change is genuine or not?

5 From Letter 46. What are the areas of compatibility that you desire in a romantic relationship that are non-negotiable for you?

6 From Letter 47. Why might it not necessarily be the best to marry someone you have been sexually active with or have become pregnant with?

7 How have you seen God's forgiveness expressed in your life? How have you seen God's forgiveness and "second start" positively affect a couple you know?

Week 8: Concluding Thoughts
Letters 49–52

From Letter 49. How do you think you would feel if marrying a particular man meant not being able to pursue something you had always dreamed of?

From Letter 50. As you read the seven pieces of "advice" proposed, comment on or discuss each one and the level of importance you would way it should have. What other principles would you propose if you were giving the advice?

- Go slow:

- Vital Christian:

- Sexual purity:

- Good provider:

- Man you will respect:

- Approval from trusted family and friends:

- Potential as a father:

3   From Letter 51. If you were to list, in order, what most relationships today are built on in our culture, consider these categories: Convictions, Character, Considerations, Chemistry. How would you rank each one and why?

4   From Letter 52. What are some of the main truths you are taking away from your study of this series of letters?

Appendices

Appendix 1

Desired Characteristics List

List the ten top characteristics you desire in a mate and start praying for God to give you such a person. Pray also that He will give you the discernment and strength to wait for such a person.

Start at the top with the "non-negotiables" (such as: he is a strong committed Christian) and go from there. Draw a double line between the "non-negotiables" and the "really important to me" items (such as: loves the outdoors).

1.

2.

3.

4.

5.

6.

7.

8.

9.

10.

Appendix 2

A Note to Fathers Raising Boys

Letter to My Daughters was not titled "Letters to My Sons" because I had none—and, these were actually personal letters to my girls. However, the characteristics mentioned in the letters are almost all applicable to young men as well. Those that are not specifically applicable are almost always talking about the characteristics of a desired man, and therefore will hopefully be instructive as well.

I am passing along below some comments to me from one dad on how he and his son used *Letters*.

> "My son, Colin, and I met for devotions every Tuesday and Thursday morning for almost 8 years—up until he graduated from high school and then left for college at the US Military Academy, West Point.

> "During his sophomore and junior years in high school, I had a very specific focus for our devotions together: we read a chapter or part of a chapter each Tuesday and Thursday from *Letters to My Daughters*. In addition, we read through a series of chapters of the Bible. Interweaving those two books gave us a balance of God's word and a dad's heart.

> "As a dad myself, it was intriguing to debrief after each devotion with my teenage son, what you had written to your teenage daughters. I saw in Colin a series of 'ahas' that developed regarding dating, giving his heart away, and wanting to more fully understand the backgrounds of young ladies with whom he might develop a serious relationship. In short, my son learned the value of searching for the hearts of other men's daughters through your tender thoughts, written concerns, and stated principles."

Appendix 3

Note to Young Men

Hey, I know it is hard to have this book in your hand. It's a bit like being seen going into a chick flick by your football teammates.

I hope you see this book not as a "chick book" but as a window into a girl's heart and what a girl's dad really wants more than anything for his daughters. Having another guy take your daughter out—let alone marry her—is pretty big. I hope you will give this book a try. Wrap it in another book cover if you must, or hide it under your mattress. For your sake, and for the sake of young women out there, I wish for this book to help you be the man God designed you to be.

Hey—here are the thoughts of a West Point cadet, reflecting on his "read" of the book.

> "The time that my dad and I spent in *Letters to My Daughters* during our Bible studies gave me insight into the heart of a dad, and is a great word picture of God's love for us. Paul Friesen's words of advice and encouragement to his daughters helped me process through some of the most demanding times of my life in high school—and all along, he points us to our true Dad. I gleaned important life lessons from this book, all the while feeling encouraged and lifted up."

Acknowledgments

Special thanks to Guy and Barbara Steele, who take any of our rough offerings and make them "look good." We deeply appreciate your expertise in editing and design.

Special thanks to Christine Kerns for her guidance on the design of the discussion guide.

Special thanks to Gabe Garcia for his contributions and suggestions for this guide. I deeply appreciate your heart for the Lord and His truth.

Thanks also to those listed below who have given suggestions for questions and/or contributed the stories that introduce each letter's study questions. Your embracing of this project and your "real life" stories mean a great deal to me: Rebecca Aeschliman, Liz Aleman, Milena Casillas, Brian and Heather Dietz, Dan and Lois Frasier, Lisa Friesen, Gabe and Kari Garcia, Beth Hendricks, Jalisa Jackson, Julie and Derek Johnson, Jeannie and Nate King, Bob and Carol Kraning, Doug and Julie Macrae, Dennis and Susan Mansfield, Colin Mansfield, Johnie Moore, Erin Moore, Dan and Wendy Taylor, David and Kassidy Thomas, Grant and Emily Williams, Danny and Stacia Woodhead, and Kate Wylie.

Anytime my fingers hit the computer keys, it is a result of life experiences with and input from our three daughters and two sons-in-law. Thank you, Kari, Lisa, and Julie, for your choices in relationships and mates. Thank you, Gabe and Derek, for being men whom I am able to trust fully with the protection, care, and love of our daughters. Lisa, thanks for not "settling." We look forward to God's provision for you in a mate if this is His best for you.

Bun, thanks for being my partner for 35 years of marriage. I love you and am so thankful for your patience with me when I have not been what I should be, and for your willingness to urge me to become all God desires me to be. I am especially thankful for your input in our girls' lives. You are an incredible model of a Godly wife and mom.

Finally, I am thankful that the Holy Spirit is able to take these words and make them become applicable to so many in so many different situations. May God be honored by this work.

About the Author

Dr. Paul Friesen and his wife, Virginia, were married in 1976 and are the parents of three young women, two of whom are now married to wonderful, Godly men. They have been involved in Family Ministries for over 35 years through family camps, church staff positions, speaking, consulting, and writing.

As the lead resource couple at Home Improvement Ministries, the Friesens regularly speak at marriage, men's, and women's conferences in the US and internationally, as well as local family and parenting seminars, and have an ongoing ministry with several professional athletic teams. Paul and Virginia both have Doctorates in Marriage and Family Therapy from Gordon-Conwell Theological Seminary.

The Friesens are (with four others) co-authors of the book *Restoring the Fallen* published by InterVarsity Press. Home Improvement Ministries published Paul's book *Letters to My Daughters* in 2006, his book *So You Want to Marry My Daughter?* in 2007, Virginia's book, *Raising a Trailblazer: Rite-of-Passage Trail Markers for Set-Apart Kids* in 2008, and Paul's book *Before You Save the Date* in 2010. They have also co-written two couple-and-small-group marriage guides, *In Our Image: Marriage as a Reflection of the Godhead* (2008) and *Jesus on Marriage* (2012).

Paul and Virginia's greatest joy in life is knowing that their children are walking in the Truth.

Other resources available from Home Improvement Ministries:

Parenting

Raising a Trailblazer, Virginia Friesen. (book)
Parenting by Design, Paul and Virginia Friesen.
 (DVD series, with study guide)
The Father's Heart, Paul and Virginia Friesen.
 (DVD series, with study guide)

Dating, Engagement

Letters to My Daughters, Paul Friesen. (book)
Before You Save the Date, Paul Friesen. (book)
So You Want to Marry My Daughter?, Paul Friesen. (book)
Engagement Matters, Paul and Virginia Friesen. (study guide)

Marriage

Restoring the Fallen, Earl and Sandy Wilson, Paul and Virginia
 Friesen, Larry and Nancy Paulson. (book)
In Our Image, Paul and Virginia Friesen. (study guide)
Jesus on Marriage, Paul and Virginia Friesen. (study guide)
Recapturing Eden, Paul and Virginia Friesen.
 (DVD series, with study guide)
Created in God's Image, Paul and Virginia Friesen.
 (DVD series, with study guide)

Discipleship

Gospel Revolution, Gabriel Garcia. (book)

~

For more information about Home Improvement Ministries, or to book
Paul and Virginia Friesen for a speaking engagement, or to order any of our
products, please contact us:

Call:	781-275-6473
Fax:	781-275-6469
E-mail:	info@himweb.org
Write:	Home Improvement Ministries
	209 Burlington Road, Suite 105
	Bedford, MA 01730 USA
Online:	www.HIMweb.org/books (for the online bookstore)
	www.HIMweb.org/speak (to book the Friesens for speaking)
	www.HIMweb.org/fb (to reach us on Facebook)

TPS 120755